A STEP BY STEP BOOK ABOUT
TROPICAL FISH

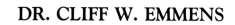

DR. CLIFF W. EMMENS

Overleaf:
Megalamphodus sweglesi, Swegles's tetra.

Photography: Dr. Herbert R. Axelrod; J. Elias; Dr. Stanislav Frank; Michael Gilroy; H. Hansen; Dr. Karl Knaack; Aaron Norman; H.J. Richter; Andre Roth; David Sands; Edward C. Taylor; J. Voss; Ruda Zukal.

Drawings by Andrew Prendimano.

Distributed in the UNITED STATES by T.F.H. Publications, Inc., One T.F.H. Plaza, Neptune City, NJ 07753; in CANADA to the Pet Trade by H & L Pet Supplies Inc., 27 Kingston Crescent, Kitchener, Ontario N2B 2T6; Rolf C. Hagen Ltd., 3225 Sartelon Street, Montreal 382 Quebec; in CANADA to the Book Trade by Macmillan of Canada (A Division of Canada Publishing Corporation), 164 Commander Boulevard, Agincourt, Ontario M1S 3C7; in ENGLAND by T.F.H. Publications Limited, Cliveden House/Priors Way/Bray, Maidenhead, Berkshire SL6 2HP, England; in AUSTRALIA AND THE SOUTH PACIFIC by T.F.H. (Australia) Pty. Ltd., Box 149, Brookvale 2100 N.S.W., Australia; in NEW ZEALAND by Ross Haines & Son, Ltd., 18 Monmouth Street, Grey Lynn, Auckland 2, New Zealand; in SINGAPORE AND MALAYSIA by MPH Distributors (S) Pte., Ltd., 601 Sims Drive, #03/07/21, Singapore 1438; in the PHILIPPINES by Bio-Research, 5 Lippay Street, San Lorenzo Village, Makati Rizal; in SOUTH AFRICA by Multipet Pty. Ltd., 30 Turners Avenue, Durban 4001. Published by T.F.H. Publications, Inc. Manufactured in the United States of America by T.F.H. Publications, Inc.

CONTENTS

Introduction

The presumed ancestors of today's fishes first appeared in the seas about 500 million years ago. Amazingly, they resembled quite closely a simple creature found today—the lancelet *(Amphioxus)*. The lancelet, about 6" (15 cm) long, is a filter feeder with a flexible rod in its back, the notochord, from which the backbone of fishes and other vertebrates has developed. By about 400 million years ago, creatures with bones had appeared, but the first true fishes are found as fossils in rocks around 350 million years old. Many different species have been found with recognizable "fishy" characteristics such as fins, a backbone surrounding the notochord, teeth and sometimes scales. Fishes were the first vertebrates; the others—amphibians, reptiles, birds and mammals—followed later, in that order.

It often seems to be assumed that the cartilaginous fishes, the ancestors of sharks and rays, were also ancestral to the bony fishes, but that does not appear to be the case. Instead, a split occurred quite early in fish evolution and some bony fishes gradually lost bony tissue and became cartilaginous. The advantage was perhaps a lighter body weight and greater flexibility. They are still mostly confined to the sea, whereas bony fishes invaded fresh waters and became their main vertebrate inhabitants. Our freshwater aquarium fishes are therefore bony fishes—so are nearly all of our marine ones.

Of the 20 thousand species available, a selection of those suitable for the home aquarium still amounts to around 5000 species, of which many hundreds are to be found in pet shops. These are in general the fishes that are attractive, usu-

FACING PAGE;
Two species that are believed to be more primitive in origin than most other aquarium fishes. The upper fish is the snakehead *Ophicephalus micropeltes.* The individual shown is a young fish and still colorful; as it matures it will gradually lose its attractive coloration. All of the snakeheads are big, voracious and tough. The lower fish is the arowana, *Osteoglossum bicirrhosum,* which grows to over two feet long.

ally colorful, reasonably hardy and not growing too large. Many of them have never seen their native waters, but have been bred and reared in commercial or hobbyists' tanks. The world-wide aquarium fish trade is enormous, involving tens of millions of fishes annually. New species are being found regularly and our capacity to breed old and new species is expanding all the time.

A long-finned form of the popular zebra danio, *Brachydanio rerio*. The upper fish is an egg-laden female. Long-finned zebra danios do not exist in nature and are cultivated in captivity for the aquarium trade.

BEING A FISH

You and I and all mammals and birds are warm-blooded and regulate our temperature within a narrow range. Fishes are cold-blooded and their temperature depends on that of the water surrounding them. Very fast, active fishes like marlin have a temperature a little above that of the water because of their muscular activity, but fishes in an aquarium don't do enough to achieve this effect. This fact has several consequences. First, a fish depends on you to regulate its temperature and it will become sick if you don't keep it within its nor-

Long-finned white cloud, *Tanichthys albonubes.* One of the easiest of all egg-laying species to propagate, the white cloud is a hardy and peaceful species that does best in water cooler than that used for more truly tropical fishes. It is a member of the family Cyprinidae.

mal range. Second, its appetite, unlike ours, rises with temperature up to a point, usually about 80°F (27°C), when oxygen shortage begins to depress it again. Third, its general metabolism (rate of body processes) also rises with temperature and so it not only eats more, if available, but excretes, moves and breathes faster.

Wild mammals and man are poor converters of food into flesh; when growing, about 10 units of food, by weight, are needed to put on one unit of flesh. Some domestic animals do better than that, having been selected for rapid growth, but fishes are the tops. They normally convert around 50% of food to flesh and so need a nutritious but quite meager diet by our standards to grow and to remain healthy. However, a starved or semi-starved *young* fish just ceases to grow or grows very slowly, and will even reach sexual maturity at a fraction of the

Regular partial changes of the water in an aquarium are of great benefit to the fishes. Such changes can be made manually or through the use of equipment available at pet shops.

normal weight. But a starved adult fish will of course go skinny, as it cannot shrink its skeleton etc. down to a juvenile state.

So the rules for keeping fishes differ considerably from those for keeping rabbits or cats or finches. Add to this that in an aquarium they cannot get away from pollution caused by urine, feces, uneaten food or other sources of toxins and we see that careful maintenance is needed. Follow the recommendations given in any good book on aquarium keeping and your fishes should remain healthy and look their best. Don't overfeed, don't overcrowd, don't allow big temperature changes to occur suddenly. Do practice regular maintenance procedures such as water changes, removal of mulm (residues on the bottom from feces, uneaten food, even plant decay), checks of pH (water acidity or alkalinity) and attention to filters and airstones.

FEEDING FISHES

Your pet store is full of fish foods, dried, frozen or alive, and it is up to you to make a wise choice from them and perhaps to supplement them occasionally from elsewhere. Many of the tougher fishes can survive on dried foods but all do better with at least some frozen or better still some live food now and then. For breeding, a rich diet including live foods is almost essential if good results are to be obtained.

Dried foods (flakes, granules or freeze-dried) should have a protein content not less than 45%. Flakes should be fairly thick and not powdery, should float and then gradually sink if uneaten and not cloud the water. Freeze-dried brine shrimp, krill, bloodworms, etc. are among the best values for the money and can contain up to 65% protein. Whichever foods you use, purchase them from a pet shop and not from a variety store.

Frozen foods, sometimes pre-sterilized, are also good, but contain a lot of water and so on a weight-for-weight basis are rather expensive compared with dry foods. They can never contain 45% protein because of the water content of up to

There are many different commercially prepared fish foods available, in a number of different forms: frozen, freeze-dried, granulated, flaked, tableted, etc. Providing fishes with a variety of different foods increases the chances of making sure that they receive good nutrition.

80%; it is their equivalent dry weight that matters, so expect 9 or 10% protein at best.

Live foods that are usually available commercially include brine shrimp, adult or to be hatched out from "eggs", white worms or mikroworms, *Daphnia* and Tubificids. You can cultivate white worms or mikroworms at home, or Grindal worms, intermediate in size between the two. Follow the methods outlined in many texts. If really enthusiastic, you can catch your own *Daphnia,* the water fleas, and some other foods such as insect larvae, but be careful to avoid pests like dragon-fly larvae and do not collect from ponds containing fishes, or disease may follow.

Do not overfeed. Give only as much as will be totally consumed within five minutes and siphon off any that remains. Feed small fishes at least twice daily and quite frugally each time, but see that they all get some, particularly bottom feeders.

KEEPING FISHES HEALTHY

If you follow the recommendations about maintaining an aquarium given in larger T.F.H. books dealing with setting up an aquarium and keeping it going, your fishes should remain in good health. A well-kept fish has a natural resistance to disease, but in the confines of an aquarium it may be subject to stresses that make it susceptible or be assailed by a massive attack introduced by a new fish. It may be weakened by toxins like ammonia, present because of overfeeding or poor maintenance, or by fumes from a domestic spray. It may be chilled by a powercut or heater failure. Such happenings can cause a healthy fish to break out with a disease it would otherwise resist. So can stress brought on by overcrowding, bullying or the wrong water conditions.

When disease does unfortunately occur, prompt treatment is usually required and some form of medication is indicated. There are plenty of proprietary remedies available in your pet shop, some good, some not, but it is necessary to decide if possible what is wrong with your fishes before taking action. Then, if a remedy contains the right amount of a recommended medicine, use it, otherwise get your own made up.

Heaters are valuable pieces of aquarium equipment, and considering the important function they perform they are relatively inexpensive.

Remember that while medication is in use, carbon filters must be turned off and biological (e.g., undergravel) filters turned down or off for short periods. Aeration should usually be increased.

Here are some of the more common causes of disease, covering perhaps 90% of the conditions likely to be encountered, and the best ways to combat them. The drugs recommended are generic. Your pet shop can offer brand name drugs.

Velvet *(Oodinum)* is caused by a protozoan (one-celled animal) that has a free-swimming stage that settles down in the gills or on the body and fins and looks like a fine rusty coating on the fish, often hard to see. The fishes scratch themselves on rocks etc. and respire heavily. The best treatment is copper sulphate (the blue crystals) in a 1% solution in distilled water. Add one standard teaspoon (5 ml) per 12 gallons (45 liters) of aquarium water on 2 successive days and a third dose on day 5 and raise the temperature to 80°F (27°C).

White spot *(Ichthyophthirius)* is caused by another protozoan with a rather similar life cycle, and causes similar be-

11

havior. It appears on the body and fins as tiny white spots, easier to see than velvet. Treat with quinine hydrochloride or sulphate at 2 grams per gallon (30 mg per liter) of aquarium water. Dissolve the necessary amount in a pint or two of water and add half of it now and the rest next day. One repeat treatment may be given, but no more or plants may suffer, and then give several partial water changes. Avoid the commonly recommended malachite green as it kills some tetras and stains plastics and silicones.

Skin cloudiness *(Costia* or *Chilodonella)* is caused by other protozoans and may be accompanied by scratching and gasping. Treat with acriflavine (trypaflavine) or monacrin (monoaminoacridine) using a 0.2% solution and giving up to one teaspoon (5 ml) per gallon. If symptoms persist, it is *Chilodonella,* so increase the dose to 4 teaspoons per gallon and give subsequent water changes. These remedies turn the water yellowish or bluish, the color fading in a few days.

The filtration equipment on the market today represents excellent value and is available in a variety of different types; shown is one of the filters known as power filters, which are miniature water pumps.

White patches under the skin *(Plistophora)* or large cysts on the body *(Glugea* etc.) are not easily cured and the affected fishes should be destroyed to prevent spread of the condition.

White fungus *(Saprolegnia* etc.) attacks weakened or injured fishes and forms a network under the skin and breaks out as tufts looking like cotton wool. Individually affected fishes are best removed to a 30-second bath of zinc-free malachite

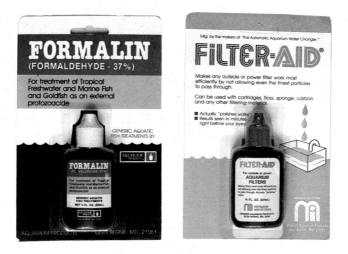

Aquarium hobbyists are able to take advantage of the many remedies and preventives that have been formulated specifically for use with tropical fish. A number of the more common aquarium fish diseases, such as ich, are easily cured with inexpensive preparations.

green at 4 grains per gallon (60 mg per liter). The green-stained fungus should drop off later. If the whole tank is affected, use a 1% solution of phenoxethol at 2 tablespoons per gallon (10 ml per liter).

Brown cysts about 1/10″ (2.5 mm) in size or smaller are caused by another fungus *(Ichthyosporidium* or *Ichthyophonus)* that invades the body via the gut and breaks out anywhere. Infected fishes are best destroyed as the disease is advanced by

the time it is seen. Then treat the tank with phenoxethol as above. It may also be added to the food to attack fungus in the gut.

Red pest, fin and tail rot are caused by various bacteria and show up as blood streaks on body and fins, ulceration and even loss of fin material. Treat mild cases with acriflavine or monacrin as for *Costia*. Severe infections need antibiotics *by mouth,* mixed up to 1% powder in the food for at least 10 days. The best is chloromycetin (chloramphenicol), but tetracyclines, gentamycin or ampicillin may be used.

Mouth fungus *(Chondrococcus)* starts as a white line around the mouth and then develops tufts, but of bacteria, not true fungus. It is one of the bacteria sensitive to penicillin, and as it is highly contagious and lethal and the fishes cannot usu-

Fishes vary in their degree of susceptibility to diseases, with some being more resistant to certain diseases and less resistant to others. Livebearers like the mollies shown here are usually more susceptible to ich than to velvet, for example, whereas other species (Siamese fighting fish, for instance) are more susceptible to velvet than to ich.

Some diseases are almost exclusively associated with certain relatively small groups of fishes. The disease known as hole-in-the-head disease, for instance, rarely affects fishes other than large cichlids. The discusfishes (shown here is the discusfish *Symphysodon aequifasciata aequifasciata*) are especially susceptible to hole-in-the-head disease.

ally eat, the penicillin should be added to the aquarium water at 40,000 units per gallon (10,000 units per liter) with further doses at 2-day intervals until a cure is effected. Chloromycetin at 50 mg per gallon may be used instead.

Flukes *(Gyrodactylus* etc.) may occasionally attack tropical freshwater fishes and can be confused with white spot, as they are only about ¹⁄₂₅" in length. Look for movement and two black eyespots. Trichlorofon (Neguvon, Bayer) at 0.25 mg per liter is a new treatment that needs only a single dose and disinfects the tank as well.

Nomenclature

This volume will introduce some of the more popular freshwater aquarium fishes, with particular attention to those

that can be kept in small communities of mixed species. Mention will be made, however, of some of the more attractive species that are best kept on their own or in specialist tanks, either because of their behavior or particular requirements. Most people start aquarium keeping with a collection of mixed species and only some specialize later on in particular species or groups.

Although many articles and books describe fishes by their popular names rather than by their systematic or scientific names, this can lead to confusion. Such names differ from place to place, even within the same language, and so we are often uncertain as to which fish is meant. So although common American and English names will be used, the systematic name of each fish will always be given as well. Hence it needs explanation.

Groups of very similar fishes anatomically are placed together in *genera* (singular *genus);* the genus is always given as the first name of a fish—rather like an oriental surname, placed first. Each individual species then receives its *specific* name to make up the binomial system of nomenclature intro-

Formerly known as *Pelmatochromis kribensis,* this fish is now called *Pelvicachromis pulcher*—but it has retained the "kribensis" portion as its common name.

duced by Linnaeus, a Swedish botanist, in the mid-18th century. So the neon tetra is *Paracheirodon innesi,* belonging to the genus *Paracheirodon* and named after Innes, the well-known American aquarist. Specific names can refer to a characteristic of the fish, such as *Hyphessobrycon flammeus,* the flame tetra, to somebody connected with it, as with Innes, to where it came from or to anything the person who names it chooses. Once a species has been referred to in a publication, and as long as no confusion can arise, it may be referred to further as, for example, *P. innesi* or *H. flammeus.*

Regrettably, scientific names do change, because of internationally accepted rules, such as that the first specific name given to a fish must take priority. So when it is discovered that our old favorite, *Pelmatochromis kribensis,* was first described by Boulenger and called *Pelvicachromis pulcher,* we have to refer to his nomenclature. If a later survey of the group to which it belongs leads to the decision that the genus should be renamed, the specific name *pulcher* will be retained. Some books give lists of previous names; often many exist for any one fish.

Livebearers

The livebearing fishes (family Poeciliidae) as their name suggests, bear living young. They are among the hardiest of aquarium fishes and among them are some of the easiest fishes to keep and to breed. No wonder that they are old-time favorites to be highly recommended for beginners. The male has an organ, the gonopodium, with which he shoots packets of sperm into the female. These can survive in many species for months and can give rise to several broods, born typically at around monthly intervals. In other species a few young are born every few days.

The young are born well developed and soon swim to whatever shelter is available, but are usually attracted to light and to the protection of surface plants. In a community tank, few if any will fail to be eaten, but some of them can easily be saved and grown up in another tank. They are mostly large enough to feed on newly hatched brine shrimp or microworms. If so inclined, you can start your own strains of a favorite species by selecting the specimens you choose for further breeding, but you must do this when they are very young, by procedures described in specialist books.

A quartet of livebearers from Central and South America is the guppy, molly, swordtail and platy, all long domesticated and available in many mutant and hybrid forms.

The guppy, *Poecilia reticulata,* was originally a species with drab females and variably colored, short-finned males. Now it has been developed into many strains of long-finned brightly colored males, with quite a bit of color in the females as well in some cases. Guppy clubs and commercial producers have given us fishes that would astonish the older aquarists,

FACING PAGE:
Deservedly among the most popular of the livebearing species is the prolific and colorful guppy, *Poecilia reticulata.* Two male guppies are shown in this photo; females would be larger and less colorful and would possess no gonopodium.

with males to about 1½" (4 cm) and females over 2" (5 cm) long. The males have long flowing fins and tails of almost any color and pattern, sword-tails, delta-tails, veil-tails, lyre-tails and so forth. Although a hardy fish, for best litter size and growth suitable live food for adults and young is recommended.

The molly, closely related to the guppy, comes in three species. The common molly is *Poecilia sphenops,* with short fins. A black variety is the most popular. This is the easiest molly to keep, but it is less hardy than the guppy and like all other mollies, does best in hard, alkaline water. The sailfin molly is *P. latipinna,* with a magnificent dorsal fin in the best specimens, available in many mutant varieties—albino, marbled, black, lyretail and so on. It is not a beginner's fish and needs room and careful handling. So does the larger Yucatan sailfin, *P. velifera,* otherwise a very similar fish. Both guppies and mollies can live in full strength sea water if gradually acclimatized to it.

The swordtail, *Xiphophorus helleri,* has a beautifully long sword in the wild-type male that is lost to some extent in some of the more colorful domesticated strains. His lady has no sword, but is equally well colored.

Hybrids with the platy, *X. maculatus,* are common. The latter is an equally popular fish with the same good qualities—hardy, peaceful, prolific and available in many varieties, but without a sword. Deeply pigmented specimens of both species and their hybrids are liable to develop melanotic tumors and are best avoided.

The sunset platy, *X. variatus,* has drab females but colorful males that do not show their full colors until adulthood. It is very hardy and can stand cool water and will overwinter in mild climates in outdoor ponds. As might be expected, many crosses are around with *X. maculatus* that do not necessarily share this attribute.

Swordtails and platys do not stand sea water, although they like a little salt in alkaline, medium hard water. They can, however, live in community tank conditions with a pH around neutral and soft water, but are not at their best in such circumstances. Swordtails can grow to 4" or 5" (10-12 cm), platys to about 3" (7½ cm), but they are usually seen much smaller.

Some other livebearers merit brief mention. The genus *Limia* has been absorbed by *Poecilia* but has left its mark in the common names of a number of fishes. The blue limia, *P. melanogaster,* is a very lively little fish, reaching about 2″ (5 cm) at most. The humpbacked limia, *P. nigrofasciata,* is of similar size and has the drawback of needing a temperature over 77°F (25°C). *Quintana atrizona,* the black-barred livebearer, is a minute fish about 1″ (2½ cm) long, not very colorful, but an old favorite. *Phallichthys amates,* the merry widow, has equally tiny males but females up to 3″ (7½ cm). These and other species were more popular decades ago but are not in favor today because more colorful species predominate.

A male swordtail, *Xiphophorus helleri.* This individual is a green swordtail, fairly close in coloration and markings to the original wild swordtail.

CYPRINIDS

The genus *Barbus* (family Cyprinidae) gave the name barbs to a group of fishes now placed in various other genera. Most come from India and the Far East with a few from Africa. They are all egg-laying fishes, nearly all easy to keep, colorful and peaceful. Many species have males that differ in appearance from females and so are readily paired off for breeding, which is typically easy to achieve. The eggs are dropped during a mating chase around the tank and no further interest is taken in them except to eat them if allowed to do so. The young are tiny on hatching and need very small live foods such as infusoria and microworm young, but can sometimes take newly hatched brine shrimp. They *can* be started on suspensions of egg yolk or yeast, but less successfully.

The new genus *Puntius* contains some old favorites. The rosy barb, *P. conchonius,* has glowing males and less colorful females, but is a very hardy and popular species, able to withstand cold conditions. A long-finned variety is quite spectacular, but needs a higher temperature. The black ruby barb, *P. nigrofasciatus,* is a beautiful fish when in color, as it fortunately usually is, but again with duller females. *P. lineatus,* the striped barb, is another pretty fish, not so often seen but well worth acquiring when you have the chance. The dwarf barb, *P. gelius,* so-called only because most other species exceed its 1½" (4 cm) length, is attractive although not brightly colored and very easy to keep and breed. Another beauty is the golden barb, *P. sachsi,* that has the same good points and is also fairly small. There are half a dozen other *Puntius* species of aquarium size and suitability, any of which are worth having.

FACING PAGE:
A pair of tiger barbs, *Capoeta tetrazona,* during a spawning chase. This colorful, fast-moving species is an old favorite among aquarists.

A male rosy barb, *Puntius conchonius*, in breeding colors.

Various striped barbs belong to the genus *Barbodes*. The six-banded barb, *B. hexazona*, has six vertical stripes and is not very brightly colored, while the five-banded barb, *B. pentazona*, is brighter and easier to breed. The two are often confused and may in fact be varieties of the same species. The larger *B. everetti*, the clown barb, is much more beautiful but is a plant eater. The spanner or "T" barb, *B. lateristriga*, can get big, up to 8" (20 cm), but is attractive although just a black and silver fish. Beware of the tin-foil barb, *B. schwanenfeldi*, often sold small but growing into an attractive but far too large fish—up to 14" (35 cm).

We come now to the third genus, *Capoeta*, into which the barbs are placed and which contains some of the best and most popular species. *C. tetrazona*, the tiger barb, with its four stripes is the best known, widely kept because of its attractiveness and despite being a fin nipper. In-breeding has resulted in various color varieties, including albinos. The banded barb, *C. partipentazona*, is a similar fish, but less colorful and not very often available. The cherry barb, *C. titteya*, my favorite barb, is a real beauty, always nicely colored but with spectacular males

Barbodes schwanenfeldi, the tin-foil barb—popular at a small size.

in season, glowing a deep red. *C. oligolepis,* the checker barb, rivals it when at its best but is usually duller in color although an excellent community fish, peaceful and hardy. Another rival is *C. melanampyx,* the ember barb, in which normally reddish males and duller females both become red in season, the males very bright red.

The cherry barb, *Capoeta titteya,* more peaceful and easier to maintain than some of the larger barb species but just as colorful.

DANIOS

Also in the family Cyprinidae, the danios come from India and the Far East, forming a small group of active, slim fishes. The zebra danio, *Brachydanio rerio*, is a small fish with horizontal black stripes or rows of dots, best kept in schools. It is a favorite fish and deservedly so, peaceful, always in motion, easily bred and very hardy. Its non-adhesive eggs must be caught when breeding the fishes by a device that allows them through, but not the fishes. A tank lined with marbles or pebbles or any fine grid will do the trick. *B. nigrofasciatus,* the spotted danio, has bars and spots and is a less popular but similar fish, in habits and breeding. So is *B. kerri,* another small and attractive fish not often seen. The pearl danio, *B. albolineatus,* is a somewhat larger fish but still only some 2½" (6 cm) at most, and well worth having. It spawns just like the others and the eggs should be caught in the same way. There is also a golden variety.

The delicate good looks of the pearl danio, *Brachydanio albolineatus,* combine with the fish's ease of maintenance and spawning to make it a favorite.

Rasbora heteromorpha, one of the smallest of the *Rasbora* species and definitely among the most desirable.

RASBORAS

Still belonging to the Cyprinidae, the rasboras, coming mostly from the Far East, are more delicate for the most part, but peaceful and often attractive fishes. A long-standing favorite is *Rasbora heteromorpha,* the harlequin fish, small and peaceful although somewhat difficult to breed unless in very soft water. It is quite tough and very attractively marked. The scissor-tailed rasbora, *R. trilineata,* is another favorite, popular because it is also hardy, active and readily bred, not because of any great brilliance of color. It does not require very soft water for breeding, but hard water does not suit it.

There are about two dozen aquarium species of *Rasbora,* most of which look best and fare best in schools. Not all are particularly attractive, but mention must be made of *R. agilis,* the black-striped rasbora, which has red in the stripe as well, *R. borapetensis,* that also has a black stripe, but a red tail, *R. dorsiocellata,* the hi-spot rasbora, with its black spot on the dorsal fin and green and gold body, and *R. einthoveni,* the brilliant rasbora, my own favorite. The Singhalese firebarb, *R. vaterifloris,* from Sri Lanka, has outstandingly brilliant males when under good conditions and is well worth obtaining.

TETRAS

Many of our most popular fishes are saddled with names that no longer relate to their systematic names. The tetras are a good example as they have undergone a double change. Many were first classified under the genus *Tetragonopterus,* which was abandoned, but the name "tetra" has stuck. They were also placed in the family Characidae, and the alternative name "characin" has also stuck. Now they belong to a group of families, including the Characidae, and are referred to as characoids.

The tetras, or characoids, are often possessed of an adipose fin, a small knob behind the dorsal fin, and many of the males have hooks on their anal fin. Most come from South America and none are found in Europe, Asia or Australia. They are egglayers and very fond of their own eggs as appetizers, so the spawning pair or trio must be removed as soon as they have finished. The young hatch out in a day or so and need very fine initial foods. There are many species, mostly small, peaceful and hardy and hence good aquarium fishes, preferring soft, acid to neutral water and quite unsuited to hard, alkaline conditions. Old favorites, as with many domesticated fishes, have been bred for mutant forms such as long fins or albinism.

The best-known tetra must surely be *Paracheirodon innesi,* the neon tetra, sold by the millions. It is a brilliant little fish that defied breeders until it was realized that it must be bred in very soft water and a dim light. The cardinal tetra, *P. axelrodi,* is an even more striking but otherwise similar fish requiring the same conditions for breeding. Both species, like many other tetras, look best and do best in schools.

Glowlight tetras, *Hemigrammus erythrozonus,* are a favorite of mine, with translucent bodies and a brilliant red stripe, first introduced in the 1930s with the neon tetra. Other

FACING PAGE:
Cardinal tetras, *Paracheirodon axelrodi,* are colorful and peaceful, so they are excellent candidates for the decorative community aquarium.

attractive members of the genus are *H. ocellifer,* the head and tail light fish, with its bright spots as indicated, and *H. pulcher,* the garnet tetra, sometimes known as the poor man's rasbora because it looks a bit like *R. heteromorpha.* At present-day prices, the rasbora is the poor man's garnet tetra!

The bloodfin, *Aphyocharax anisitsi,* is an exception to the rule for characoids—it does well in hard alkaline water although being quite happy in soft water too. *Serrasalmus* species are another exception, this time to the general rule that characoids are peaceful or fairly peaceful fishes. The genus includes the famous piranhas, prohibited imports in many countries.

The pencilfishes of the genus *Nannostomus* are peaceful, sometimes timid, and rarely exceed 2″ (5 cm) in length—in other words, mostly excellent aquarium fishes, looking best in schools. *N. beckfordi,* Beckford's pencilfish, *N. marginatus,* the dwarf pencilfish, *N. trifasciata* and *N. unifasciatus,* the three-lined and one-lined pencilfishes, are particularly recommended, but only the dwarf pencilfish is really happy as a community member.

Among other small species to be particularly recommended are *Pyrrhulina vittata,* the banded pyrrhulina, *Thayeria boehlkei,* the penguin fish, *Copella arnoldi,* the splash tetra and *Carnegiella strigata strigata,* the marbled hatchet fish. The two last-named are jumpers, the splash tetra when spawning and when guarding the eggs, the hatchet fish at any time. The splash tetra is an exceptional characoid in that the pair when spawning deposit the eggs above water, on a leaf or such, and the male continues to splash them until they hatch. Then no further care of them is taken.

Passing to larger fishes, we have the Anostomidae, characoids known as headstanders because of their typical head-down stance. The striped headstander, *Anostomus anostomus,* is the best-known and most striking, but grows to 8″ (20 cm) and must be avoided. The lisa, *A. taeniatus,* gets to only 5″ (12½ cm) and is a nice example of the family. Various *Leporinus* species that like to eat vegetable matter are of a similar build, but are not such constant head-standers. Suitably sized for a medium to small aquarium are *L. pellegrini,* Pellegrin's lep-

This is *Nannostomus beckfordi,* one of the colorful but relatively unheralded pencilfishes.

orinus, a black-spotted fish, and *L. striatus,* which grows to 12″ (30 cm) in nature but stays smaller in the aquarium.

Other attractive characoids are *Exodon paradoxus,* the bucktoothed tetra, which unfortunately fights its own species, but is peaceful with others; *Copeina guttata,* the red-spotted copeina, which grows larger in the fish tank than in nature, a rare occurrence, and *Phenacogrammus interruptus,* the Congo tetra, with its weird ragged-looking fins and tail. All tend to grow to a fair size but can be kept down to be accommodated in a medium-sized tank.

CATFISHES

Catfishes, naturally, have whiskers, hence the name. However, this causes all kinds of whiskered fishes to be grouped together, although they belong to different and often unrelated families. The armored catfishes of the family Callichthyidae are in general small "stony" fishes that include the well-known *Corydoras* species. The sucking catfishes of the family Loricariidae are used as algae eaters and as "uglies" in the aquarium. The family Siluridae supplies the popular "glass" catfishes, the family Mochokidae the upside-down catfishes, and so on.

The corydoras, from South America and Trinidad, are small, peaceful, bottom-living fishes with hard external bony plates that must make it difficult to eat them. They are much in demand as scavengers and will clean up an infestation of tubifex in the aquarium better than any other fish. There are many species. The bronze corydoras, *Corydoras aeneus,* was an early introduction that has now been largely replaced by more attractive species. These include the leopard corydoras, *C. julii,* the skunk corydoras, *C. arcuatus,* and the blue corydoras, *C. natereri,* all of a 2"-3" (5-7 cm) size. The pygmy corydoras, *C. hastatus,* is only about 1½" (4 cm) long at most and is an exception to the general rule in that it swims up into the water. The corydoras have a complicated mating ritual that finishes up with the female depositing eggs in batches on various hard surfaces in the tank.

Other callichthyid fishes such as *Callichthys callichthys,* the slender armored catfish, grow much larger, up to 8" (20 cm) or more and are bubblenest builders, the male guarding the eggs until hatching.

The Loricariidae are also South American in origin and for aquarium purposes the family includes some potentially

FACING PAGE:
Synodontis angelicus, an African catfish of the family Mochokidae, is one of the more strikingly patterned catfish species—and one of the most sought after.

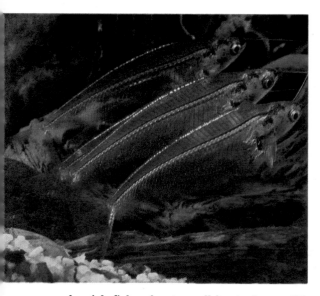

Kryptopterus bicirrhis is a very delicate-looking catfish species and is very peaceful as well.

largish fishes kept small by tank conditions. They are attractive because of ugliness rather than any other characteristic. Arnold's sucker catfish, *Otocinclus arnoldi,* is an exception, growing only to about 2″ (5 cm), and so is the whiptail catfish, *Loricaria parva,* reaching only about 4″ (10 cm). The bristle-noses, various *Ancistrus* species, do not grow above about 6″ (15 cm)

Corydoras aeneus, the most common of all catfish species seen in aquariums, is an all-around fine aquarium fish.

This close-up of an *Ancistrus* species shows exactly why those loricariid catfishes are known collectively as bristle-noses.

and can be kept smaller. They are not often available but are so ugly, particularly *A. lineolatus,* that they are well worth having!

The glass catfishes, *Parailia* and *Kryptopterus* species, of which *K. bicirrhis* is the most transparent, show varying degrees of glassiness and in contrast to most catfishes. *K. bicirrhis* swims in mid-water for choice. Its transparency, with a silvery sac enclosing the gut, makes it an attractive although rather delicate fish, best kept in schools.

The upside-down catfishes, genus *Synodontis,* actually vary in the extent of the habit of swimming the wrong way up. *S. nigriventris,* the most consistent upside-downer, is not a very attractive fish except for its unusual habit. But at least it only grows to about 4" (10 cm), whereas many of its more colorful relatives get much larger. A favorite, although rare and rather large, is *S. angelicus,* the polka-dot upside-down catfish, which doesn't swim upside-down very much but looks magnificent.

Members of the many other families of catfishes are mostly too large when fully grown for a medium-sized tank and require aquaria in the 4' to 6' (120-180 cm) range. They are often available as small fishes, but if you are attracted to one, look it up first!

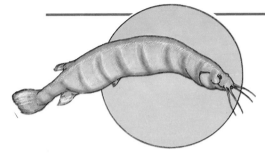

LOACHES

The best-known of the family Cobitidae, the loaches, are no doubt the coolie loaches, *Acanthophthalmus* species. They are bottom-living scavengers, happiest in groups, and if in a well-planted tank they will sometimes surprise their owner by producing young. The true coolie loach, *A. kuhli,* has practically full vertical bands on the body, *A. myersi,* the slimy myersi, has very broad full bands, *A. semicinctus,* the half-banded loach, has them on the top only and *A. shelfordi,* Shelford's loach, has rows of blotches rather than bands.

Perhaps the next best known to the coolie loaches are the various members of the genus *Botia,* of which the clown loach, *B. macracantha,* is the most impressive. With its bold pattern of black and yellow, plus reddish fins, it is an outstanding fish. It likes its own company and looks best in small schools that swim very actively about the tank. Although it can grow to 12″ (30 cm), it is usually sold much smaller and remains so in the usual set-up. *B. hymenophysa,* the banded loach, is another beauty; however, it grows too large and predatory and must be avoided in stocking a small tank.

Other attractive and more reasonably sized botias include the orange-finned loach, *B. modesta,* and *B. sidthimunki,* the dwarf loach. The first-named is rather rare and very shy, whereas the second is the opposite in character and grows only to about 1½″ (4 cm) in length. All botias are difficult to breed, but some success has been achieved with the clown loach recently.

The spined loach, *Cobitis taenia,* or weatherfish, is almost a cold-water fish but can stand tropical conditions as well. It is quite a prettily marked fish and a good scavenger, but should be fed properly. It used to be believed that it changed its swimming habits according to the weather. Another weatherfish is *Misgurnus anguillicaudatus,* which is not a cold-water fish, nor it is attractive. The barred loach, *Noemacheilus fasciatus,* looks like a fatter coolie loach, but is a rather aggressive fish with quite different habits.

Less often seen than its more colorful cousin the clown loach, *Botia hymeno-physa* also is an attractive fish, but it's more pugnacious than *B. macracantha*.

KILLIFISHES

The family Cyprinodontidae includes hun dreds of species of small, often very decorative fishes with the habit of frequenting and breeding at the top of the water, in among plants. Others, however, lay eggs at the bottom, particularly in situations where the pond is liable to dry up. A characteristic of the top minnows, or killifishes, is the production of eggs that may take days, weeks or even months to hatch, and can be dried without being killed. They have been hybridized to a considerable extent, but rarely to advantage. You do not see them too often in shops, but many societies exist devoted entirely to them. The top minnows nearly all need frequent feeds of live foods to do best and failing that, frozen foods of a suitable size.

Many of the most beautiful species occur in the genus *Aphyosemion*. This genus, in fact, contains some of the most colorful fishes known and it is a pity that they are on the whole rather touchy fishes, best kept on their own or with similar species, usually requiring soft, well-aged slightly acid water. They then spawn readily onto floating plants or mops and the eggs are collected, or the fishes may be moved from tank to tank and the eggs left to hatch, as egg-laying is normally fairly continuous over a lengthy period. It has been found that with some species it is best to give them a rest at the end of each two weeks or infertile eggs may be laid.

Some examples of the choicest species follow, but there are many others. Ahl's lyretail, *A. ahli,* like many other *Aphyosemion* species, comes in various color strains, from yellowish through green to blue bodies with multicolored fins. The lyretail, *A. australe,* has a beautiful tail, as the name indicates, and beautiful colors, but only in the male, as with most other *Aphyosemions.* The two-striped aphyosemion, *A. bivittatum,* is a fairly hardy favorite and equally colorful; so is *A. cognatum,* the red-spotted aphyosemion. Many aphyosemions have red spots or bars but *A. cognatum* has them so dense that it appears red from a distance.

The panchaxes, genus *Epiplatys,* offer tougher but less

striking fishes than the aphyosemions, but there are some very pretty species. However, those that grow fairly large should not be kept with small fishes, which they will eat. The red-chinned panchax, *E. dageti,* formerly *E. chaperi* and often sold as such, is an old favorite, hardy, colorful and fairly easy to breed. The spotted panchax, *E. macrostigma,* and the striped panchax, *E. fasciolatus,* are also recommended species, but the latter is a jumper and must be kept well covered.

It is a pity that the genus *Nothobranchius,* which has some very colorful fishes, is mostly to be shunned because they are nearly all too pugnacious. *N. rachovi,* for example, is one of the best but must be kept on its own and be fed on live food. Mention must also be made of the genus *Cynolebias,* of which *C. bellottii,* the Argentine pearl fish, is the best known. These are short-lived little fishes that inhabit seasonal water holes and lay eggs that dry up during part of the year as the rains cease. During this period, no fishes exist, and the eggs hatch out with the next rains. If kept in an aquarium, the adults will live for a year but not much longer.

A male lyretail, *Aphyosemion australe,* one of the colorful and easy-to-breed killifish species.

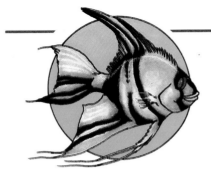

CICHLIDS

Fishes of the family Cichlidae are notable for caring for their eggs and young and rarely do they eat them. Many are far too large and too pugnacious for an ordinary community tank, but a relatively few are small and peaceful, even large and peaceful, and can be kept with other fishes. The best-known older cichlids came mostly from Central and South America, but quite recently there has been a horde of new species from Africa, from lakes that had previously been unexplored commercially. These include some beautiful species, but they are not for the community tank, or even for other than experienced aquarists. As I am writing for the beginning aquarist rather than otherwise, we shall consider mainly cichlids that can be kept with other fishes. Breeding habits will be considered briefly under each group.

The angel fish, *Pterophyllum scalare,* has been kept for a long time and is now a polymorphic species—meaning that there are many color and finnage varieties. To mention some, there are black, golden, silver, marbled, veiltail, lace, longfinned angels, and of course combinations of color and finnage. A naturally longfinned angel, *P. scalare altum,* is imported occasionally and a very handsome fish. *P. dumerili,* the only other recognized angel species, is rarely seen and is almost indistinguishable from *P. scalare,* but doesn't grow as large.

The angel fishes go through quite a courtship, with a wrestling match in typical cichlid fashion, and lay their eggs on large leaves, rocks or even the aquarium glass. Both parents fan them and when the fry hatch they are transferred from pit to pit dug in the gravel. Later, they are guarded meticulously by the parents until old enough to fare for themselves.

Discus fishes, various *Symphysodon* species and strains, have also been around for a long time, some 50 years, but were not bred in any numbers until it was realized that the

FACING PAGE:
Not highly colorful but definitely attractive and graceful, the angel fish is one of the most desirable of the cichlid species and has long been regarded as an aquarium standard.

Good looks and small size are joined with a relatively peaceful disposition to make *Apistogramma ramirezi* probably the most popular "dwarf" cichlid.

young feed from mucoid secretions of the body of both parents. They are mentioned for that reason, and because they are handsome fishes, but they are large and touchy and not for beginners, although quite peaceful.

The dwarf cichlids, growing only to about 2½" (6 cm), are peaceful, colorful and excellent community fishes. The genus *Apistogramma* provides some of the best species; the only drawback is that if you have a pair that spawns, the female becomes very aggressive and chases even the male away and will damage or kill him if they are left together. The butterfly cichlid, *A. ramirezi,* is a beautiful multicolored fish, doing best in soft, acid water and on live food. It is timid rather than aggressive and should not be with boisterous tankmates. Another popular fish is Agassiz's dwarf cichlid, *A. agassizi,* with similar habits and requirements. Reitzig's dwarf cichlid, *A. reitzigi,* has long flowing fins in the male and is a real dwarf, not exceeding 2" (5 cm) in length. The male gets a rock surface ready for

spawning and then the female takes over and chases him off after the eggs are laid. Most of the remaining *Apistogramma* species are best kept on their own and it is wise to choose from those just mentioned for your tank of mixed species and for safety to have just a single, more colorful male of each species chosen. In a different genus, the golden dwarf cichlid, *Nannacara anomala,* is attractive and peaceful, except when spawning or guarding the young. The checkerboard cichlid, *Crenicara filamentosa,* is another pretty and peaceful dwarf.

Although not classed as a dwarf, the kribensis, *Pelvicachromis pulcher* (originally *Pelmatochromis kribensis,* hence the name), is not much larger and is a beautiful, peaceful fish. As with the dwarfs, the female becomes aggressive when guarding eggs and young, so get just a male unless you want to breed them—in a separate tank. A relative, the striped kribensis, *P. taeniatus,* is not often seen and is so like the kribensis that it is likely to be offered as such. Both are African fishes, so unlike their usually fierce brethren from that continent.

Among the larger, more characteristic cichlids peaceful or relatively peaceful species just crop up here and there, usually in genera that are far from peaceful as a rule. They include the firemouth, *Cichlasoma meeki,* which looks fierce but isn't. It is a beautiful fish growing only to about 4″ (10 cm), with a

A male *Cichlasoma meeki,* the firemouth, one of the mid-sized cichlid species.

spectacular red belly and chin in the male. A relative, *C. festivum,* the flag cichlid, is also peaceful but gets a bit larger and less tolerant when fully grown. Two other worthwhile, relatively small and peaceful members of the genus are *C. aureum,* the golden cichlid, and *C. sajica,* the T-bar convict fish. Nearly all other *Cichlasoma* species are pugnacious or too large or both. The genus *Aequidens* offers a few similar exceptions, such as the flag cichlid, *A. curviceps,* which stays at about 3" (7½ cm) and is quite decorative, *A. maroni,* the keyhole cichlid, a little larger but still acceptable, and *A. itanyi,* the dolphin cichlid, which unfortunately pulls up plants and so is a dubious candidate.

The orange chromide, *Etropus maculatus,* from India and Sri Lanka, is another small and attractive cichlid that usually stays peaceful, but there are exceptions. Its relative, *E. suratensis,* the banded chromide, is a rogue and grows large. The only drawback to the orange chromide is that it really does best in slightly salty water that can be hard on plants although harmless to many other fishes.

Although you will possibly never keep them, the African lake cichlids deserve more than just a mention. Why won't you keep them? Because nearly all come from very alkaline water (pH 7.7 to 9.2) and are pugnacious. There are hundreds of new species, so far mostly coming from Lakes Malawi and Tanganyika. Those from Lake Malawi are mostly mouthbrooders, whereas the Tanganyika cichlids usually spawn in a typical cichlid fashion. The Malawi cichlids include over a hundred species of *Haplochromis,* some of which are very colorful. Outstanding are *H. burtoni,* Burton's mouthbrooder, in which the female takes the eggs into her mouth, and *H. moori,* the blue lumphead, colored as indicated and with a lump on the head. Even more colorful are the mbunas, falling into several genera, some of which are polymorphic (coming in several color forms). *Pseudotropheus tropheops,* the tropheops, and *P. zebra,* the zebra, for instance, come in any color from near white, to yellow, blue, golden, brown, speckled or barred or just plain colored.

In Lake Tanganyika are cichlids with an enormous range of sizes as well as color varieties. They range from 1½" (3.5 cm) to over 3 ft (90 cm). *Tropheus moorii,* the moorii,

Cichlids

comes in over 30 colors, including olive, green, brown, black, blue-black, yellow, red, some striped and some not. The genus *Lamprologus* does not offer species with such variability, but has many members that have become aquarium favorites. The smallest species, of various genera, have become popular since some are shell dwellers, occupying snail shells, while others are called goby cichlids because of their goby-like habits. *Spathodus erythrodon,* the blue-spotted goby cichlid, is said to be peaceful and easy to keep, but it still needs hard, very alkaline water. It is a mouthbrooder, in contrast to most other Tanganyika species.

A pair of *Melanochromis auratus;* the male is the blue fish. This mouthbrooding African cichlid species (formerly called *Pseudotropheus auratus*) is one of the more commonly available Lake Malawi fishes.

ANABANTOIDS

These fishes are distinguished by the possession of an organ called the labyrinth, used to absorb oxygen from air gulped in at the surface of the water. It is rich in blood vessels arranged over thin plates of tissue to give optimum performace. The anabantoids are dependent on the labyrinth and will drown if not given access to the air. The organ enables them to live in foul water, in which typical members of the group build bubble nests from a sticky saliva secreted by the male. He then entices ripe females to accompany him below the nest and embraces them as they spawn and the eggs are fertilized. Then he swims down and catches as many eggs as possible in his mouth and spits them into the nest. After spawning he drives the female off and cares for the eggs until hatching and in some species he even guards the fry.

One of the first foreign fishes kept in Europe was the paradise fish, *Macropodus opercularis,* and was probably the fish referred to by Pepys in his famous diary. It can stand cold water and regrettably, since it is a handsome fish, it is quarrelsome and not for the community tank. Its relatives, *M. cupanus cupanus,* the spike-tail paradise fish, and *M. cupanus dayi,* Day's paradise fish, are in contrast peaceful and although not as striking are well worth keeping.

The famous Siamese fighting fish, *Betta splendens,* is another anabantoid, quite safe in the community tank if only one male is present, or if females are kept. Two males will fight until one or both are severely damaged or one is killed. The fighter has been extensively inbred and some of the most gorgeous freshwater fish have been produced—long finned and of

FACING PAGE:
A male pearl gourami, *Trichogaster leeri,* under
his bubble nest. Pearl gouramis are excellent
aquarium fish.

many colors; mostly combined with reflecting cells called irido-
cytes that give a metallic sheen to the fish. Females remain
short-finned, but are also colorful. The male builds a typical
bubble-nest and the breeding display is well worth watching.
There are many relatives of *B. splendens,* some fairly peaceful
but none as decorative as the domesticated species.

Fighting bettas are bred in the Orient for gambling,
short-finned and ferocious. All bettas may be kept in quite
small vessels, as a visit to your aquarium shop will demonstrate,

A male Siamese fighting fish, *Betta splendens;* a female of the species would
have much shorter fins and would be less colorful.

as they are usually displayed in jam jars or the like, since the
decorative males cannot be placed together. However, this
does not mean that the fish are best so kept; they should be
given plenty of space in permanent quarters once you take
them home.

The gouramis, in contrast to the foregoing fishes, are
generally peaceful and may be kept together or with other
fishes. Probably the most popular is the pearl gourami, *Trichogaster leeri,* which is shy rather than otherwise. It is a lovely,
delicate-looking fish with a lacy pattern of black, white and vio-
let, and an orange colored belly in the male at mating. In keep-

ing with its appearance, the fish is not aggressive even when breeding, when it produces a large number of eggs that may be gently guarded by both parents. The three-spot gourami, *T. trichopterus,* that can get rather large at 6″ (15 cm) or so, has been ousted in its original wild form by a blue cultivated strain, the blue gourami, a very popular fish. There is also a gold gourami, another variant and a handsome one too, and the Cosby gourami, to my thinking less attractive, with broken vertical stripes. To complete the list of common gouramis we must add the snakeskin gourami, *T. pectoralis,* which although peaceful grows far too large at 8″ − 10″ (20-25 cm).

In contrast to the above, we have two small species, of the genus *Trichopsis.* The pygmy gourami, *T. pumilis,* does not get much larger than 1″ (2½ cm) long and is so shy that it is best kept on its own, but it is a ready breeder and a pretty fish. Its cousin, *T. vittatus,* the croaking gourami, gets to about 2½″ (6 cm), and is also shy. Its croak is heard, if you listen carefully, during spawning. Both species need a high temperature, around 80°F (27°C) and 84°F (29°C) for spawning. The dwarf

A pair (the male is the upper fish) of one of the color varieties of *Trichogaster trichopterus,* the three-spot gourami.

gourami, *Colisa lalia,* named before *T. pumilis* was discovered, grows only to about 2″ (5 cm) and is normally quite shy, but my daughter has a rogue that chases its tank-mates quite viciously! The male is a beautiful little fish with enameled-looking blue and red vertical stripes and is exceptional in that he incorporates bits of plants and other materials into his bubblenest. Other *Colisa* species are also peaceful and decorative. The honey gourami, *C. chuna,* and the thick-lipped gourami, *C. labiosa,* both stay small, but the "giant" gourami, *C. fasciata,* gets to about 5″ (12½ cm).

A male dwarf gourami, *Colisa lalia.* This good-looking anabantoid fish is usually in good supply.

In this trio of kissing gouramis, one fish has already attached its mouth to the side of another, while the third appears to be waiting its turn to do the same.

Another large gourami, the kissing gourami, *Helostoma temmincki,* gets up to 12" (30 cm) long, but is often sold quite small and grows rapidly, to the dismay of its owner. The kissing habit, not only of each other but almost anything else, is of uncertain significance. The list of gouramis could be continued, but we shall close it with a mention of the chocolate gourami, a small fish with a long name, *Sphaerichthys osphromenoides.* This is because after a long period of doubt it is now established that it is a mouthbrooder—holding the eggs and young in the mouth instead of building a bubblenest.

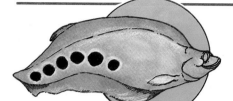

OTHER FAMILIES

There are lots of other fishes suited to the community tank, some quite rarely seen and worth buying when available, others commoner, but cropping up here and there in different families so that it is hardly feasible to list each family separately. Unless otherwise mentioned, those listed here do not exceed 4" (10 cm) in length and can be housed in medium sized aquaria. We shall take them in alphabetical order.

Badis badis badis, the dwarf chameleon fish from India, is a pretty little fish with a pattern of iridescent colors; it must usually be given live foods and is a bit shy. So try it if you feel that it will be happy under the conditions and with the company you can provide for it.

Butis butis, the crazy fish from the Far East, is a real oddball, an upside-down goby that cleans algae from any surface, but likes live food as well. It can grow to 6" (15 cm) but is reported not to worry smaller fishes.

Chanda baculis is the smallest of the glassfishes, usually referred to as the Burmese glassfish, and rarely exceeds 2" (5 cm). It is really transparent and does well in soft water, in contrast to its relatives, *C. buroensis,* the Siamese glassfish and *C. ranga,* the "common" glassfish, which require some salt in the water and are not so transparent.

Epalzeorhyncus kalopterus, the flying fox from Sumatra and Borneo, is a real gem. It is peaceful, beautiful and omnivorous and a good algae eater—what more could we want? *E. siamensis,* the Siamese flying fox, is almost as attractive and has the same habits, but is very rarely available.

Garra taeniata, the Siamese stone-lapping fish, is an-

FACING PAGE:
Chanda ranga, one of the glassfishes—the blue edging on the fins becomes most noticeable if the fish is maintained in alkaline, salty water.

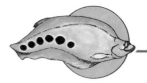

other attractive omnivore that is also an algae eater. Although it comes from fast-flowing streams it does well in the aquarium, but does prefer slightly alkaline water. It can also grow to around 6″ (15 cm), but would rarely do so in a smallish tank. Not often seen, it is worth purchasing when available.

Labeo bicolor, the red-tailed shark, is a very territorial fish and can be a bad bully.

Labeo bicolor, the red-tailed shark from Thailand, and *L. erythrurus,* the rainbow shark, are both beauties. *L. bicolor* has a black body and a red tail, with black fins. It is peaceful to other species but has a tendency to bicker with its own, particularly if two males are together. It is usually offered quite small, but can grow to 5″ (12½ cm) in a large tank. *L. erythrurus* has reddish fins as well as tail, but is not usually as jet black as *L. bicolor.* It is otherwise of similar habits and size. Both species

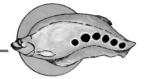

Melanotaenia macullochi, an atherinid species from Australia, is non-aggressive and easy to care for in addition to being good-looking.

prefer somewhat alkaline, hard water (around 200 ppm), but I have kept them successfully in soft water and so have other aquarists. Beware of other *Labeo* species, offered as small inoffensive-looking fishes, as they can grow very large and sometimes quite aggressive. The *Labeo* species belong to the family Cyprinidae, but they are listed here separately because the aquarium trade only rarely groups them with the barbs and rasboras and danios.

Melanotaenia macculochi, the dwarf Australian rainbow fish, is a pretty and peaceful fish, normally quite colorful but with splendiferous males when spawning. It is only about 2½″ (6 cm) long and a very hardy creature. Other, larger members of the genus include *M. splendida,* the pink-tailed Australian rainbow fish, which needs a larger aquarium to flourish and grows to about 5″ (12½ cm), and *M. nigrans,* the dark Australian rainbow fish. Of the many other Australian or New Guinea rainbows, *M. coatesi,* Coates's rainbow fish, and *M. boesemani,* Boesman's rainbow fish, merit special mention as being fairly small and very colorful.

Monocirrhus polyacanthus, the leaf fish, from South America, is found in slow streams, drifting like a dead leaf and

Not often seen on the market but usually appreciated for its oddness when available is the butterflyfish, *Pantodon buchholzi.*

waiting for unwary prey. The resemblance to a leaf in color and form is quite remarkable, even to a mid-vein and a lower lip resembling the stalk. Do not put it in with small fishes as it will swallow them and is hardly therefore a very suitable community fish, but you may like it as a rare curiosity. Feed it on live food as it grows; it wil not exceed 4″ in length.

Mogurnda mogurnda, the Australian purple-striped gudgeon, is another pretty fish regrettably best kept on its own or with larger fishes. But if you do happen to have a tank of robust fishes, this gudgeon makes a fine addition to it, but do not put it in with long-finned or slow-moving specimens—it is a fin nipper.

Pantodon buchholzi, the butterfly fish, is another oddity that has the advantage of being trainable to eat other than its normal diet of live insects. If kept with fishes that are not likely to damage its long ventral filaments it can be an interesting addition to the tank. This should be kept well covered as the butterfly fish can glide over the water and out of the tank.

Pseudomugil signifer, the Australian southern blueeye, is an active, peaceful small fish that can accommodate itself to community tank conditions but actually looks its best in alkaline, even brackish water, where it usually lives. Then it colors up splendidly and turns from a pretty little fish to a real beauty, growing to about 2½″ (6 cm). There are several other quite tiny *Pseudomugil* species, some not very prepossessing, but of them, *P. gertrudae* is well worth having, although growing only to about 1″ (2½ cm) or a little more. Some other species from New Guinea, which do not seem to have been imported, are spectacular.

Rhadinocentrus ornatus, another Australian rainbow fish, is active and peaceful, liking a little salt in the water but doing well without it, as do many of the Australian fishes, some of which are euryhaline, meaning tht they can pass from fresh to salt water with no trouble, or vice versa.

Scatophagus argus, the spotted scat, is a fairly attractive fish from the Indo-Pacific, but the tiger scat, *S. argus* var. *rubifrons,* is a beauty. The young are produced in estuaries that may be practically fresh, although the adults are marine fishes. At about 1-1½″ (2½-4 cm) the young fishes adapt well to a community tank, although a little salt helps, and will remain

Kept under conditions that bring out its best, *Pseudomugil signifer* becomes a very colorful fish. Note the blue of the eyes.

The Celebes rainbow fish, *Telmatherina ladigesi*, is subtly colored and does not show to advantage unless given conditions to its liking.

small and attractive for a year or two if not overfed. As they age they gradually become less spectacular. At that stage, about 3" (7½ cm) long, I once passed a few over to the local zoo, where they were thrown unceremoniously into full seawater. A few months later I couldn't recognize them; they were about 10" (25 cm) long and ugly-looking brutes! The spotted scat can grow to 24" (60 cm).

Selenotoca multifasciata, the silver scat, comes from the same waters as the spotted scat and has similar requirements. It is an attractive fish with the great advantage that it retains its appeal and grows only to about 4" (10 cm).

Syngnathus pulchellus, the African freshwater pipefish, is peaceful and an unusual, attractive fish, but it must have live foods, although it will pick at frozen foods. If you feel you can keep it happy, remembering that brine shrimp, young and adult, are normally available, have a go. It will also accept freshwater crustaceans like daphnia, whereas its relatives, *S. spicifer,* the Indian freshwater pipefish, will not. It only accepts baby guppies in a normal aquarium. Although these pipefishes are labeled "freshwater," they need a little salt and will tolerate brackish water.

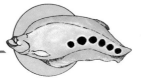

Telmatherina ladigesi, the Celebes rainbow fish, is very beautiful when mature (up to 4″ or 10 cm), when the males with gorgeous black and yellow fins are unmistakable. It is a rather timid fish and should be with suitable companions such as pencil fishes and aphyosemions, with a little salt in the water, about 1 teaspoon (5-7 g) per gallon . Salt does not make water hard or alkaline or harm other fishes, but use butchers' salt or the pure chemical, not table salt, which has unwanted additives.

Tetraodon species, or puffers as they are known, are included as a warning. You may be attracted to some of these oddballs, and be tempted to buy one, but don't! They are all aggressive and nasty, even killing other fishes.

The fishes sold under the name "freshwater puffers" may be comical looking, but they are no joke to their tankmates. The puffer shown here is attacking a shrimp, but the victim could just as easily have been a fish.

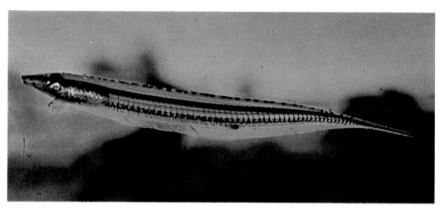

Above: The knife fishes are very interesting as a group, but some of them can be very nippy; the species shown here is *Urumara rondoni.* **Facing page:** A pair (male is upper fish) of blue platies, *Xiphophorus maculatus,* in glowing good health—the way aquarium fish *should* look.

Urumara rondoni, the mousetail knife fish from Vene-zuela, is a peaceful, unusual fish and one of the few knife fishes that stays reasonably small, usually about 4" (10 cm). It swims by undulations of its overdeveloped anal fin and can move backwards or forwards equally easily. However, it will eat small fishes and so should be kept with suitable tank-mates. It will eat ordinary live or frozen foods as well.

A FINAL REMINDER
    If you are a beginner, you are unlikely to have quaran-tine facilities at home, yet it is dangerous to introduce new fishes to an established aquarium unless they have been iso-lated for at least 2 weeks and preferably treated with a mild dis-infectant such as monacrin or acriflavine. Ask your dealer if he does this with new fishes and try to find one that does. Other-wise, find out if possible how long he has had a fish before you buy it. If he has had it for 2 weeks or more and it seems healthy you don't risk too much by purchasing it. Without these pre-cautions, look very critically at any new purchase and indeed at the whole tank for several weeks after any addition to its fishes or plants—which can also carry infections or parasites. This ad-vice may seem a little paranoid, but it is well worth taking!

That's why we advise you to buy your fishes from an aquarium or pet store.

Then remember the golden rules—**don't overcrowd, don't overfeed,** but do **practice regular maintenance** including water changes, pH checks, removal of mulm and attention to all equipment. Look critically at your aquarium every day— it only takes a minute to check the temperature, note that all is well with filters and airstones and to look for any signs of trouble—a fish missing or lurking in a corner or looking miserable. When you feed them, try to see that all the fishes are eating and behaving normally. The alert aquarist *looks* for trouble and if he finds it he does something about it as soon as possible. But if he follows the rules above, he very rarely will find it.

An aquarium doesn't have to be fancily decorated in order to be a good home to fish—but good looks don't hurt, either.

The following books published by T.F.H. Publications are available at pet shops and book stores everywhere.

HANDBOOK OF TROPICAL AQUARIUM FISHES (New Edition)
By Drs. Herbert R. Axelrod and Leonard P. Schultz
ISBN 0-87666-491-5
PS-663 (Hardcover)
5½ x 8"; 736 pages
Relied upon by many, many thousands of aquarists, this book is a classic. Covers everything.

EXOTIC TROPICAL FISHES EXPANDED EDITION
By Dr. Herbert R. Axelrod, Dr. C. W. Emmens, Dr. Warren E. Burgess, and Neal Pronek
ISBN 0-87666-543-1 (hardcover)
ISBN 0-87666-537-7 (looseleaf)
T.F.H. H-1028 (hardcover)
H-1028L (looseleaf)
The "bible" of freshwater ornamental fishes—contains comprehensive information on aquarium maintenance, plants, and commercial culture, as well as over 1,000 color photos and entries on many hundreds of species. New supplements are issued every month in *Tropical Fish Hobbyist* magazine, and may be placed into the looseleaf edition.

DR. AXELROD'S ATLAS OF FRESHWATER AQUARIUM FISHES
By Dr. Herbert R. Axelrod, Dr. Warren E. Burgess, Neal Pronek, and Jerry G. Walls.
ISBN 0-86622-052-6
T.F.H.H-1077
The ultimate aquarium book—illustrated with over 4000 color photos. Almost every fish available to hobbyists is illustrated! Species are grouped geographically and by family for easy reference. No aquarist's library is complete without it!

DR. AXELROD'S MINI-ATLAS OF FRESHWATER AQUARIUM FISHES
By Dr. Herbert R. Axelrod, Dr. C. W. Emmens, Dr. Warren E. Burgess and others
ISBN 0-86622-385-1
H-1090
Smaller in size than the large Atlas on which it was patterned but still containing over 2000 full-color photos, this book contains even more general aquarium information about setting up and maintaining an aquarium, fish breeding, disease treatment, etc. Tremendous value.

VIERKE'S AQUARIUM BOOK
By Jörg Vierke
ISBN 0-86622-103-4
T.F.H. PS-834
One of Germany's leading aquarists presents one of the most thorough aquarium books ever written, discussing virtually every aspect of aquarium keeping—much more than just fishes.

Index